Kitty Litterature

Written & Illustrated
by
Phyllis Forbes Kerr

Published by
Walrus Productions

Published by Walrus Productions
4805 NE 106th St. Seattle, WA 98125 (206) 364-4365

Written & Illustrated by Phyllis Forbes Kerr
Layout and typography by Bunky @ The Durland Group

Printed by Vaughan Printing, Nashville, Tennessee

Library of Congress Catalog Card Number 96-061371

Kerr, Phyllis Forbes.
    Kitty Litterature / Phyllis Forbes Kerr
    p. cm.
    ISBN 0-9635176-1-9
 1. Cats--Humor. 2.Cats--Humor, Pictorial.   I. Title

PN6231.c23k47 1997   818'.54
                            QB196-40434

                   Printed in the United States of America

                     10 9 8 7 6 5 4 3 2 1

Dedicated to:

My son Adam
who loves to cat pun

What do you call a cat
who knows where he's going?

A Cat with a Purrpuss

What kind of cars
do fat cats drive?

What do terrified cats suffer from?

Clawstrophobia

Why do cats
often turn and walk away?

Because you hurt
their felines

What do cats like best for dessert?

Chocolate Mouse

What do cats lie on when they nap?

Catterpillows

What do you call
a cat's large tummy?

A Cat Gut

What do you call a very fussy cat?

Purrsnickitty

What do you call
an angry cat?

1. What do you call a cat who has kittens?

2. What do you call a cat who doesn't have kittens?

LITERATE

ILLITTERATE

What do cats use
for grooming?

Catacombs

Where do kittens
order toys and other
special items from?

Catalogues

What do cats read
at bedtime?

Furry Tails

What do cats do
while they wait
for Santa Claws?

Kiss
under
the
mouseltoe

What annual social event do cats eagerly await each year?

The Fur Ball

Where do you hear
the loudest noise
in the cat orchestra?

The Purrcussion Section

An author who wrote
and illustrated
"A Tail of Tom Kitten"

Beatrix
Pawter

A famous playwright
author of
"Cat and Supercat"
"Catmalion"

George
Purrnard
Paw

A writer of the prairies
who wrote "My Catonia"

Willa Catter

An American
short story writer
who wrote
"The Kit and the Pendulum"

Edgar Allan Paw

An English author
who wrote
"Pride & Purredjudice"
and
"Purrsuasion"

Jane Pawstin

A "Dickens" of a cat novel

"A Tail of Two Kitties"

A favorite
American Cat Opera

"Pawgey & Bess"
by Cole Pawter

What ballet
is a favorite with cats?

"The Dance of the Sugar Plum Furries"

Two Great
Cat Singers

Purrtha Kitt   Cat King Cole

A classical
Cat Musician

Catgang
Amedeus
Meowzart

A well known Cat Cellist

Meow
Meow
Ya

The King Cat
of Rock 'n Roll

Elvis
Purresley

Three Cat Stars

Meow Furrow   Al Purrcino

Raymond
Furr

TV talk show host
(a late night cat)

David Litterman

A movie musical starring
Audrey Hepurrin'

"My Fur Lady"

A comic movie about three city cats

"Kitty Slickers"

A 1986 film adapted
from a novel by
E.M. Furester

Room with a Mew

A movie starring
Tom Cat Cruise

"Frisky Business"

A Very Scary
Cat Movie

An Egyptian Cat Ruler

Meowpatra

A famous Cat Explorer

Christofur
Columpuss

Two Native American Cats

Pawcahontus and Hiapawfur

An American Frontier Cat

A peanut farmer
and
former U.S. President

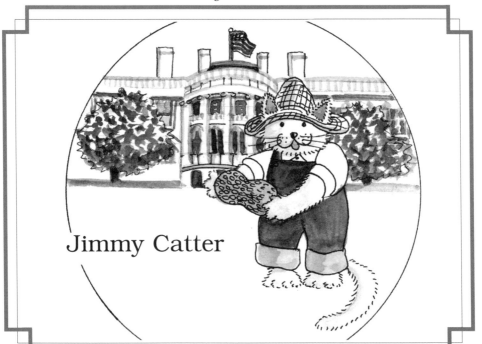

Jimmy Catter

A business cat
&
presidential wannabe

Ross Purro

A big cat in government?

"Squeaker
of the
Mouse"

A Chinese Communist Cat Leader

Chairman Meow
(Mousietongue)

Franklin D. Roosevelt was famous for...

Fireside Cats

A lithograph
by
Edvard Meowunch (1893)

"The Howl"

An oil painting of a
young musician
by
Edouard Catet (1866)

"The Fifur"

Religious art
by Fur Angelico (1450)

"The Annunciation"

A portrait
by James Whisker (1871)

Whisker's
Mother

A family portrait
by Clawed Monet (1875)

"Camille Monet and a Kitten"

A famous cat
hockey player

Gordie
Meow

One of history's best cat golfers

A super cat
basketball player

Michael
Pawdon

An Italian
Olympic skier from the
1992 Winter Games

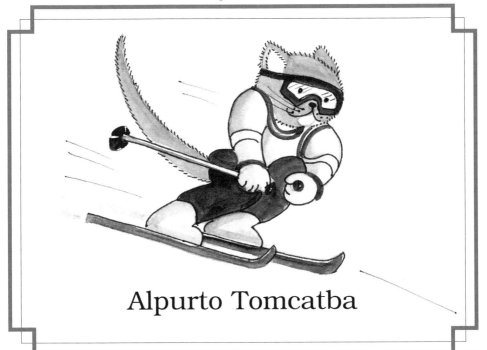

Alpurto Tomcatba

One of the greatest
cat baseball players

Stan Meowsial

A Ukrainian
Olympic skater
who won the Gold
in 1994

Oksana Meow

1996 U.S. Open
champion cat
tennis player

Pete
Sampurrs

Where do cats go bargain shopping in Boston?

"Feline's Basement"

What sound does
a sneezing cat make?

What do you call
a cat who is obedient
and well trained?

What do you call
a cat who
doesn't tell the truth?

A Lion

What do you call
a cat who
doesn't play fair?

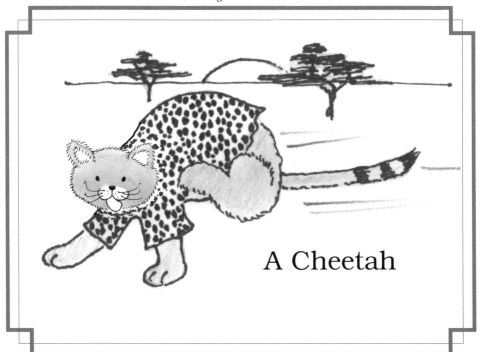

A Cheetah

What do you call it
when a cat gets
into a little mischief?

A Kittastrophy

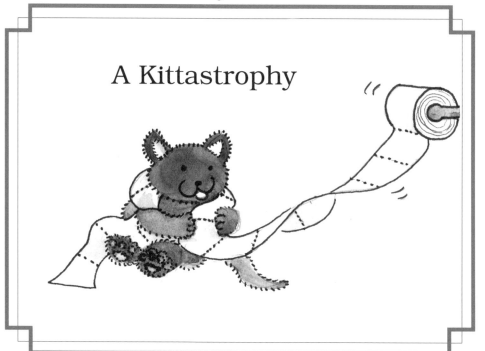

What do you call it
when a cat gets
into a lot of mischief?

A Catastrophy

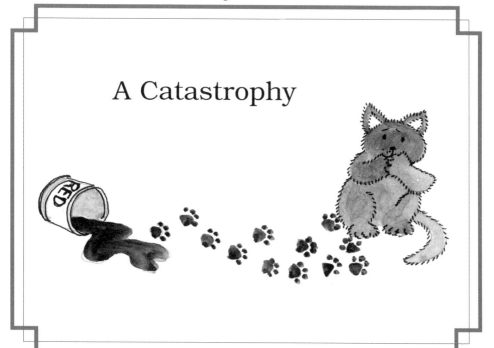

A common career chosen by cats

What do you call a cat
who reaches the top?

"CATAMOUNT"

How do cats knit?

They
Purrl

What do you call a cat
who makes lace?

A
Puddy-Tat

Where do cats go for their winter vacations?

St. Kitts

What kind of boat
do cats like best?

CATAMARANS

What do cats watch on TV?

Catoons

How are cats' towels monogrammed?

What do you call a cat
with boundless energy?

What is the name of an ancient cat weapon?

Who do cats call
when they are in trouble?

The Fur Department

Where do bad cats go when they die?

PURRGATORY

What do cats do
when they have a problem?

They ask Dear Tabby

What do you call nine cats in a row?

Cats 'n nine tails

THE END

ABOUT THE AUTHOR

Phyllis Forbes Kerr lives in Cambridge, Mousie-chewsetts with her husband Andrew, her golden retriever, Clover and tiger cat, Sparkey. She is a Wheelock graduate & former kindergarten & first-grade teacher who holds a masters degree from Lesley College as a reading specialist.

She is the author & illustrator of several children's books and most recently compiled & edited <u>Letters from China</u> (1838-1840 Canton-Boston correspondence of her great-great-grandfather, Captain Robert Bennet Forbes).

Phyllis has designed greeting cards for many years and now with her sister-in-law has a successful line of greeting cards under the name JoyPhyl Greetings.

AVAILABLE COMPANION BOOKS

Whimsical wisdom in a collection of delightful quotes to
make you think, chuckle, self-motivate & lift your spirits.

ISBN 0-9635176-0-0

ISBN 0-9635176-3-5

ISBN 0-9635176-4-3

GREAT
FOR
GIFTS

ISBN 0-9635176-7-8

ISBN 0-9635176-8-6

ORDER ADDITIONAL BOOKS AS GIFTS

KITTY LITTERATURE
ISBN # 0-9635176-1-9

Qty_____ @ 6.95 Each _____

MOTHERHOOD
is not for Wimps
ISBN # 0-9635176-7-8

Qty_____ @ 6.95 Each _____

HOW DOES YOUR
GARDEN GROW?
ISBN # 0-9635176-8-6

Qty_____ @ 6.95 Each _____

MONEY
Now You Have It. Now You Don't.
ISBN # 0-9635176-4-3

Qty_____ @ 6.95 Each _____

THE ROAD TO SUCCESS
Is Always Under Construction
ISBN # 0-9635176-0-0

Qty_____ @ 6.95 Each _____

ACHIEVE YOUR DREAMS
ISBN # 0-9635176-3-5

Qty_____ @ 6.95 Each _____

Add 2.00 for shipping for 1st book, 50¢ ea. thereafter
WA State residents only: add applicable sales tax

Total _____

Send check with order to:

Walrus Productions
4805 N.E. 106th St
Seattle, WA 98125

Name _____

Address _____

City _____

State / Zip _____

These books may be ordered through your local book store.